THE GREAT BIBLE Discovery

DANIEL, RUTH, ESTHER

THE BIBLE IS A BEST-SELLER. IT IS ALSO ONE OF THE MASTER-WORKS OF WORLD LITERATURE - SO IMPORTANT THAT UNIVERSITIES TODAY TEACH 'NON-RELIGIOUS' BIBLE COURSES TO HELP STUDENTS WHO CHOOSE TO STUDY WESTERN LITERATURE.

THE BIBLE POSSESSES AN AMAZING POWER TO FASCINATE YOUNG AND OLD ALIKE.

ONE REASON FOR THIS UNIVERSAL APPEAL IS THAT IT DEALS WITH BASIC HUMAN LONGINGS, EMOTIONS, RELATIONSHIPS. 'ALL THE WORLD IS HERE.' ANOTHER REASON IS THAT SO MUCH OF THE BIBLE CONSISTS OF STORIES. THEY ARE FULL OF MEANING BUT EASY TO REMEMBER.

HERE ARE THOSE STORIES, PRESENTED SIMPLY AND WITH A MINIMUM OF EXPLANATION. WE HAVE LEFT THE TEXT TO SPEAK FOR ITSELF. GIFTED ARTISTS USE THE ACTION-STRIP TECHNIQUE TO BRING THE BIBLE'S DEEP MESSAGE TO READERS OF ALL AGES. THEIR DRAWINGS ARE BASED ON INFORMATION FROM ARCHAEOLOGICAL DISCOVERIES COVERING FIFTEEN CENTURIES.

AN ANCIENT BOOK - PRESENTED FOR THE PEOPLE OF THE SECOND MILLENNIUM. A RELIGIOUS BOOK - PRESENTED FREE FROM THE INTERPRETATION OF ANY PARTICULAR CHURCH. A UNIVERSAL BOOK - PRESENTED IN A FORM THAT ALL MAY ENJOY.

M publishing
CARLISLE, UK

15

DANIEL, RUTH, ESTHER

Here are three of the most dramatic stories in the Bible. In different ways, each of them shows how God controls events and how loyalty to him brings its own reward. The story of Daniel is set in Babylon at the time before and after the Persians captured the city. Daniel and his three friends find themselves trying to do something very difficult. Unlike many of their fellow Jews, they are not able to live quietly, simply obeying the Jewish law. They are at the king's court where people will be aware of everything they do - or refuse to do. They serve the king well but without compromising their obedience to the God of Israel. This leads them into all sorts of danger but God protects them. No wonder this book has encouraged God's people in every age to accept responsibility in the world but to remain faithful to him.

We are all tempted to look down on 'foreigners' and the Jews were no exception. The story of Ruth shows how David, the greatest king of Israel, and the ancestor of the messiah, was himself descended from a heathen woman. In the character of Ruth it also shows a beautiful picture of loyalty. And what a coincidence that after Ruth came to Bethlehem, with her mother-in-law, she should start gleaning in the fields of the one man best able to help the two penniless women! The story is a reminder that God's people are grateful for 'coincidences' but should not be totally surprised by them.

The Book of Esther is the only one in the Bible in which the name of God does not appear. Only in 4:14 is it hinted at, when Mordecai says that help for the Jews may come 'from another place'. But like Daniel, this book is based on the belief that God is in control of events and well able to look after his people. Mordecai goes on to suggest to his niece that it may be 'for such at time as this' that she has been given her special position. When people refer to 'Providence' what they have in mind is this belief that God is in control of what may seem like chance events and that they have a place in his purposes.

DANIEL
RUTH
ESTHER

First published as *Découvrir la Bible* 1983

First edition © Larousse S.A. 1984
24-volume series adaptation by Mike Jacklin © Knowledge Unlimited 1994
This edition © OM Publishing 1995

01 00 99 98 97 96 95   7 6 5 4 3 2 1

OM Publishing is an imprint of Send the Light Ltd.,
P.O. Box 300, Carlisle, Cumbria CA3 0QS, U.K.

All rights reserved.
No part of this publication may be reproduced, stored in a retrieval system, or transmitted, in any form or by any means, electronic, mechanical, photocopying, recording or otherwise, without the prior permission of the publishers.

Introductions: Peter Cousins

British Library Cataloguing in Publication Data
A catalogue record for this book is available from the British Library
ISBN 1-85078-219-9

Printed in Singapore by Tien Wah Press (Pte) Ltd.

IN THE THIRD YEAR OF THE REIGN OF JEHOIAKIM, KING OF JUDAH, NEBUCHADNEZZAR CAPTURED JERUSALEM, DEPORTING THE PEOPLE OF JUDAH TO HIS CAPITAL CITY, BABYLON.

SCENARIO: Etienne DAHLER
DRAWING: Raymond POÏVET

DANIEL The Seer

HERE IS BABYLON!

THAT'S THE GATE OF ISHTAR!

IN NEBUCHADNEZZAR'S BEDROOM...

BUT THE MAGICIANS COULDN'T DO SO...

LOOK, THE GUARDS ARE BURNT, JUST BY GOING NEAR IT!

AT ANY RATE, WE'LL BE RID OF THOSE FOREIGNERS!

AND TOWARDS EVENING...

WHAT A MIRACLE! THEY'RE STILL ALIVE!

THEN NEBUCHADNEZZAR ORDERED EVERYONE TO WORSHIP THE GOD OF THE JEWS, AND HE HEAPED GREAT HONOURS ON THE THREE YOUNG MEN.

* Menē, menē, tekēl, upharsin.

(Daniël 5, 25)

16

DARIUS THE MEDE, KING OF THE PERSIANS, WAS CROWNED WHEN HE WAS 62 YEARS OLD.

DANIEL, BECAUSE YOU'RE A GOOD MAN, YOU'VE RISEN TO THIRD PLACE IN THE KINGDOM. FROM NOW ON YOU'LL BE MY CHIEF OFFICIAL.

ON THE EUPHRATES, DARIUS SPOKE TO DANIEL...

I'LL CHOOSE 120 SATRAPS* TO SERVE UNDER YOU...

* District governors.

...BECAUSE I'M AFRAID THAT I'LL BE ASSASSINATED.

THE JEWISH MERCHANTS WHO LIVED IN BABYLON WERE AFRAID.

OVERJOYED AT FINDING DANIEL ALIVE, DARIUS ISSUED AN EDICT.

DANIEL! ALIVE! YOUR GOD PROTECTS YOU!

I WANT TO TELL THE WHOLE WORLD THAT YOUR GOD IS THE LIVING GOD. AS FOR YOUR ENEMIES...

MANY YEARS LATER, A FAMILY WAS IN ITS HOME IN THE JEWISH COLONY OF JERUSALEM. THE FATHER WAS TELLING HIS FAMILY THE STORY OF DANIEL IN THE LIONS' DEN— AND HE CONCLUDED...

... THEY WERE EATEN EVEN BEFORE THEY TOUCHED THE GROUND. THAT'S HOW ISRAEL'S ENEMIES DIE.

IT WAS THE YEAR 170 BC. THE SYRIAN KING ANTIOCHUS IV HAD JUST BEGUN TO PERSECUTE THE JEWS VERY SEVERELY...

DANIEL WASN'T A PROPHET LIKE JEREMIAH OR EZEKIEL; HE WAS MORE OF A WISE MAN WHO COULD EXPLAIN VISIONS.

TELL US AGAIN, GRANDDAD.

DANIEL HAD FOUR VISIONS. THIS IS THE VISION OF THE FOUR BEASTS...

DURING BELSHAZZAR'S REIGN DANIEL HAD A DREAM, AND WROTE IT DOWN...

I SAW THE FOUR WINDS OF HEAVEN BLOWING OVER THE GREAT SEA, AND FOUR HUGE BEASTS CAME UP OUT OF IT...

...THE FIRST WAS LIKE A LION, BUT IT HAD AN EAGLE'S WINGS. WHILE I WAS WATCHING, THE WINGS WERE TORN OFF, AND IT WAS GIVEN A HUMAN MIND...

THE SECOND WAS LIKE A BEAR, AND IT WAS TOLD: EAT AS MUCH MEAT AS YOU CAN!

I SAW ANOTHER, LIKE A LEOPARD. IT HAD FOUR WINGS AND FOUR HEADS. IT WAS GIVEN POWER TO RULE.

THEN A FOURTH BEAST APPEARED. IT WAS A TERRIFYING SIGHT. IT HAD TEN HORNS. THREE HORNS WERE TORN OUT, AND IN THEIR PLACE A LITTLE HORN BEGAN TO GROW, WHICH HAD HUMAN EYES.

The story of RUTH
David's ancestress

Among the women honoured in the Bible, one was a foreigner from the land of Moab, who in her own way saved the people of Israel.

I'M RUINED!

ELIMELECH, EVEN IF IT RAINED NOW, IT WOULDN'T DO ANY GOOD!

DURING THE TIME OF THE JUDGES, THERE WAS A FAMINE IN BETHLEHEM...

SCENARIO: Etienne DAHLER
DRAWING: Pierre FRISANO

MY FRIEND, I'VE MADE UP MY MIND. I'M LEAVING THIS CURSED LAND!

BUT, MASTER ELIMELECH, YOU MUSTN'T RUN AWAY FROM THE LORD'S PUNISHMENT!

WE MUST STAY HERE AND PRAY TO THE LORD!

REALLY? WELL, YOU STAY! I CAN'T PRAY ON AN EMPTY STOMACH!

SEEING THAT THE FAMINE IN JUDAH WAS OVER, NAOMI DECIDED TO GO BACK TO HER COUNTRY.

MY DAUGHTERS, GO BACK TO YOUR FAMILIES... YOU'VE BEEN A GREAT HELP TO ME IN MY SORROW.

NO, MOTHER, I WANT TO GO WITH YOU!

BUT I'VE NOTHING MORE TO OFFER YOU! I BEG YOU: MAKE NEW LIVES FOR YOURSELVES HERE!

NAOMI, I THINK YOU'RE RIGHT.

I, RUTH, WILL FOLLOW YOU, MOTHER. YOUR PEOPLE WILL BE MY PEOPLE; YOUR GOD WILL BE MY GOD.

PEOPLE SAW THEM ARRIVE.

IS THAT REALLY NAOMI? SHE LOOKS SO OLD!

I DON'T KNOW HOW SHE WOULD LIVE WITHOUT HER DAUGHTER-IN-LAW.

WHILE ORPAH STAYED IN THE LAND OF MOAB, RUTH DECIDED TO GO TO JUDAH WITH HER MOTHER-IN-LAW.

...AND THEY SET OFF FOR BETHLEHEM TOGETHER.

28

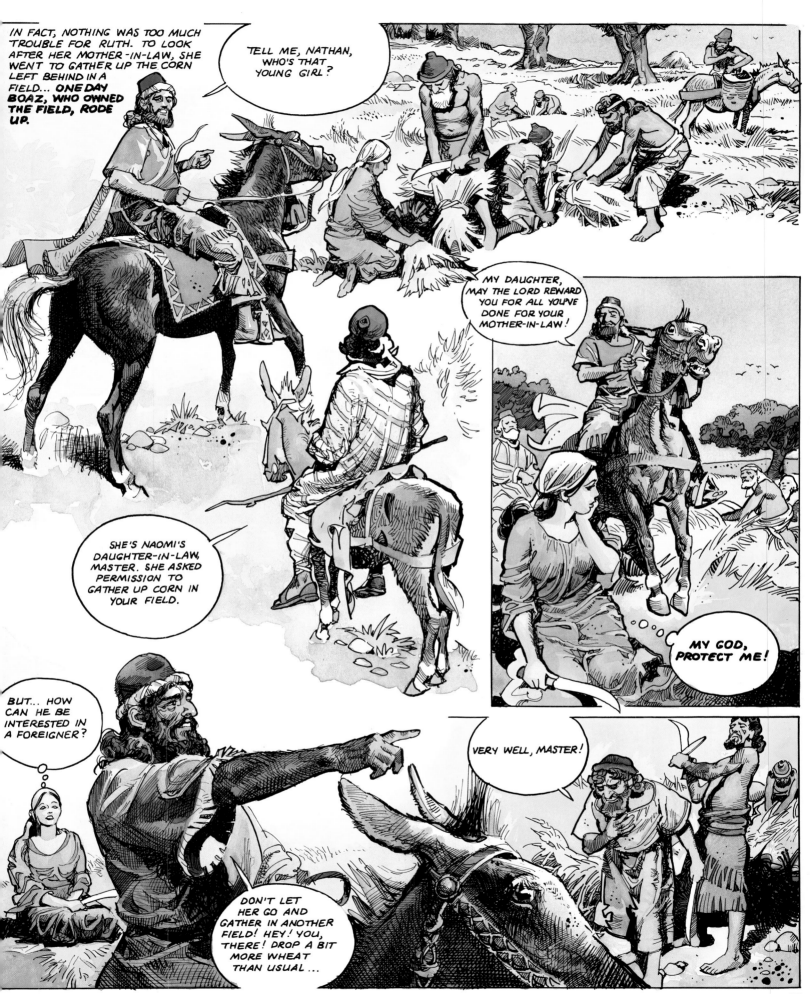

THERE'S BOAZ... HE'S ASLEEP...

THAT SAME NIGHT RUTH WENT TO THE THRESHING-FLOOR, AND DID EVERYTHING HER MOTHER-IN-LAW HAD TOLD HER.

DID YOU TAKE OFF MY SANDAL?

AREN'T YOU MY DEAD HUSBAND'S COUSIN?

THAT WILL REMIND HIM OF HIS DUTY — THAT'S WHAT NAOMI SAID...

THEN RUTH LAY DOWN AT BOAZ'S FEET...

WHAT!... WHO'S THERE?

IN THE MIDDLE OF THE NIGHT...

DON'T BE AFRAID, BOAZ. IT'S I, YOUR SERVANT RUTH.

THEN I ASK YOU TO ACT AS MY KINSMAN, AND MARRY ME.

WHEN BROTHERS LIVE TOGETHER, AND ONE OF THEM DIES WITHOUT AN HEIR, THE OTHER ONE OR HIS NEAREST RELATIVE MUST MARRY THE WIDOW. IF HE REFUSES, SHE WILL TAKE OFF HIS SANDAL, AND HIS WHOLE HOUSEHOLD WILL BE PUT TO SHAME.

(See Deuteronomy 25:5-10)

ESTHER
a woman who saved her people

SCENARIO: Etienne DAHLER
DRAWING: Pierre FRISANO

FOR JEWISH CHILDREN ALL OVER THE WORLD THE FESTIVAL OF PURIM IS STILL TODAY A TIME OF REJOICING.

SUCH AN INSULT! ... THE QUEEN SHOULD BE BANISHED!

AND YOUR DECISION WILL BE RECORDED FOR EVER IN THE LAWS OF THE MEDES AND THE PERSIANS.

SOME TIME LATER, WHEN HIS ANGER HAD COOLED DOWN, AHASUERUS BEGAN TO MISS THE QUEEN. HE SPOKE ABOUT IT TO HEGAI, THE CHIEF EUNUCH.

MEMUCAN, I LIKE THAT IDEA!

LET THE KING APPOINT MESSENGERS TO BRING ALL THE MOST BEAUTIFUL YOUNG GIRLS IN THE EMPIRE TO SUSA...

...THE ONE THE KING LIKES BEST WILL BE QUEEN IN VASHTI'S PLACE!

HADASSAH, MY DAUGHTER, DON'T LET ANYONE KNOW YOU'RE JEWISH. TELL THE MESSENGER THAT YOUR NAME IS ESTHER.

ESTHER'S BEAUTY WAS SOON NOTICED.

YOU'LL BE PERFUMED AND MADE UP BEFORE YOU APPEAR IN FRONT OF THE KING.

MEANWHILE MORDECAI HAD BEEN APPOINTED KEEPER OF THE ROYAL GATE. IN THIS WAY HE COULD KEEP IN TOUCH WITH ESTHER. THEN ONE DAY...

...MORDECAI HAS DISCOVERED A PLOT AGAINST THE KING...

I MUST WARN HIM!

THE KING'S LIFE WAS SAVED, AND THE TWO CONSPIRATORS WERE EXECUTED.

I, HAMAN, HAVE BECOME THE MOST IMPORTANT MAN IN THE EMPIRE... EVERYONE MUST KNEEL BEFORE ME, BY ORDER OF THE KING!

WHO'S IGNORING THE ROYAL ORDER BY REMAINING ON HIS FEET?

KING AHASUERUS HAD PROMOTED ONE OF HIS RELATIVES ABOVE ALL THE OTHER OFFICIALS.

MEANWHILE HAMAN'S WIFE, ZERESH...

AS LONG AS MORDECAI IS SITTING AT THE PALACE GATE, YOU WON'T BE A MAN!

BUT, ZERESH, THE HONOUR THE QUEEN IS GIVING ME — ISN'T THAT ENOUGH?

NO! ASK THE KING TO HANG MORDECAI TOMORROW MORNING... THEN YOU CAN HAPPILY GO TO ESTHER'S BANQUET.

I'LL HURRY TO THE PALACE!

THE KING COULDN'T SLEEP, SO HE ORDERED THE OFFICIAL RECORDS OF THE EMPIRE TO BE READ TO HIM.

I HAD A LUCKY ESCAPE THAT TIME! BUT WHAT WAS THE NAME OF THE MAN WHO SAVED ME? WAS HE REWARDED?

ER... HERE IT IS. IT'S MORDECAI... AND NOTHING IS SAID ABOUT ANY REWARD.

HAMAN, YOU'VE COME AT THE RIGHT TIME! TELL ME HOW TO REWARD A MAN WHO SAVED MY LIFE.

SEE WHAT'S DONE FOR A MAN WHOM THE KING WANTS TO HONOUR!

DRESSED IN ROYAL ROBES AND WEARING A CROWN, MORDECAI WAS LED THROUGH THE CITY OF SUSA BY HAMAN.